Countries Around the World

China

Patrick Catel

Heinemann Library
Chicago, Illinois

www.capstonepub.com

Visit our website to find out more information about Heinemann-Raintree books.

To order:

☎ Phone 888-454-2279

🖥 Visit www.capstonepub.com to browse our catalog and order online.

Edited by Abby Colich and Claire Throp
Designed by Ryan Frieson and Steven Mead
Original illustrations © Capstone Global Library, Ltd., 2012
Illustrated by Oxford Designers & Illustrators
Picture research by Ruth Blair
Originated by Capstone Global Library, Ltd.
Printed in China by China Translation and Printing Services

15 14 13 12 11
10 9 8 7 6 5 4 3 2 1

Library of Congress Cataloging-in-Publication Data
Catel, Patrick.
   China / Patrick Catel.
      p. cm.—(Countries around the world)
   Includes bibliographical references and index.
   ISBN 978-1-4329-6096-4 (hb)—ISBN 978-1-4329-6122-0 (pb)
   1. China—Juvenile literature. I. Title.
   DS706.C395 2012
   951—dc22   2011015258

Acknowledgments

The author and publishers are grateful to the following for permission to reproduce copyright material: Corbis pp. 19 (© Alex Hofford/epa), 27 (© Fritz Hoffmann/In Pictures); Dreamstime.com pp. 10 (© Chengxin), 17 (© Zhang Lianxun), 20 (© Goory), 21 (© Markussevcik), 23 (© Bbbar), 24 (© Hupeng); iStockphoto p. 15 (© Prill Mediendesign & Fotografie); Shutterstock pp. 5 (© gary718), 6 (© Ke Wang), 7 (© testing), 9 (© Hung Chung Chih), 13 (© Mikhail Nekrasov), 14 (© Pick), 18 (© Mike Flippo), 25, 29 (© shupian), 28 (© Cora Reed), 31 (© Maxim Tupikov), 32 (© hxdbzxy), 33 (© Teerapun), 35 (© Tan Wei Ming), 36 (© BartlomiejMagierowski), 39 (© aspen rock), 46 (© adam.golabek).

Cover photograph of a painted golden dragon reproduced with permission of Shutterstock (© konmesa).

We would like to thank Seth Wiener for his invaluable help in the preparation of this book.

Every effort has been made to contact copyright holders of any material reproduced in this book. Any omissions will be rectified in subsequent printings if notice is given to the publisher.

All the Internet addresses (URLs) given in this book were valid at the time of going to press. However, due to the dynamic nature of the Internet, some addresses may have changed, or sites may have changed or ceased to exist since publication. While the author and Publishers regret any inconvenience this may cause readers, no responsibility for any such changes can be accepted by either the author or the Publishers.

Contents

Some words in the book are in bold, **like this**. You can find out what they mean by looking in the glossary.

Introducing China

What comes to mind when you think of China? Is it dragon dances, fireworks, and the Great Wall? Or porcelain and silk? Or maybe kung fu and beautiful temples? The huge nation of China is all of those things, but also much more.

People's Republic of China

China's official name is the People's **Republic** of China. China is located in eastern Asia, and it is the fourth-largest country in the world. Although it is just a bit smaller than the United States, China has about four times more people. In fact, China has the greatest population of any country in the world, with over 1.3 billion people!

China stretches roughly 3,400 miles (5,500 kilometers) from north to south, and 3,100 miles (5,000 kilometers) from east to west. It is bordered by the Pacific Ocean on the east and south, mountains to the west, and a dry area to the northwest. China's climate includes a variety of conditions, from **subtropical** weather in the southeast to **subarctic** weather in the far north. Mount Everest is the tallest peak in the world.

The Chinese century?

China has become a powerful force in the world **economy** in recent years. Today, it is dealing with issues related to managing its large population and preserving its natural **environment**. It also faces international concerns about how it handles human rights. However, throughout these times of change, the Chinese maintain the traditions of their rich, ancient **culture** as they continue forward into the 21st century—a century many predict to be the "Chinese century."

How to say...
The Chinese traditionally call their country *Zhongguo*, which means "Middle Kingdom." This is because the ancient Chinese felt their country was the middle, or center, of civilization.

Old and new mix in today's Chinese cities, with historic temples and modern skyscrapers visible in the same photograph.

History: Ancient Civilization to Modern Power

In China, the Longshan people first appeared around 10,000 BCE. They built walls around their settlements, grew crops, and raised animals for food. These and other early peoples shaped early Chinese culture.

China was then ruled by **dynasties** for thousands of years. The first dynasty was the Xia, beginning around 2100 BCE. The Shang Dynasty followed, beginning in the 1700s BCE. There were advances in metalwork, stonework, science, and the arts during the Shang Dynasty. The first Chinese writing also appeared in this dynasty.

China's first emperor

China's first kings ruled only part of what is today China. In 221 BCE, Ying Zheng united several kingdoms and became China's first **emperor**. He took the name Qin Shi Huangdi (*Huangdi* means "emperor" and *shi* means "first"), and so began the Qin Dynasty. He set up a strong government and created standard measures, language, and **currency** throughout the empire.

Qin Shi Huangdi ordered the construction of this army of soldiers made of terracotta, a kind of clay pottery. The army was buried underground until it was discovered by a farmer in 1974.

Qin Shi Huangdi began construction of the Great Wall to keep out Mongol invaders. It was built using forced labor, and many workers died.

Later dynasties

Mongol emperors ruled China from 1279 to 1368 CE. The famous conqueror Genghis Khan (1162–1227) united Mongolian groups and created a large empire across Asia. Kublai Khan (1215–1294), a grandson of Genghis Khan, conquered China in 1279, making it part of the Mongol Empire. This was the beginning of the Yuan Dynasty. The Mongols were driven from power by the Ming Dynasty (1368–1644). This was followed by the Qing Dynasty (1644–1911), China's last dynasty.

China's dynasties

The following are approximate dates for some major dynasties that ruled China:

Years	Dynasty
1046–256 BCE	Zhou
221–207 BCE	Qin
206 BCE–220 CE	Han
581–618 CE	Sui
618–907	Tang
960–1279	Song
1279–1368	Yuan (Mongol)
1368–1644	Ming
1644–1911	Qing (Manchu)

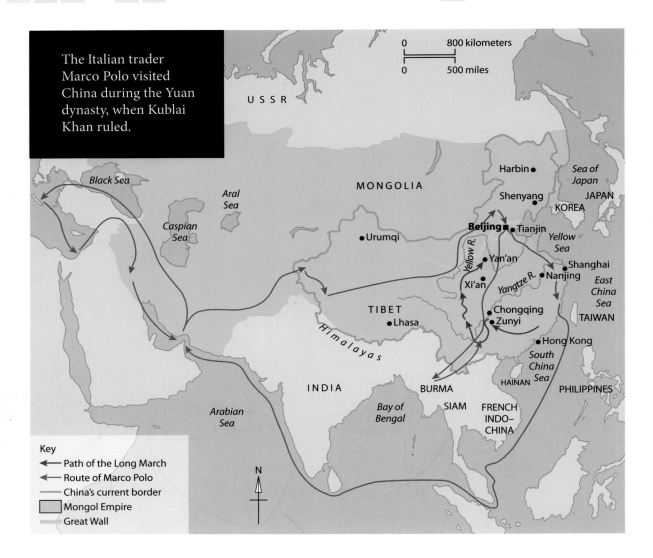

The Italian trader Marco Polo visited China during the Yuan dynasty, when Kublai Khan ruled.

Key
- ← Path of the Long March
- ← Route of Marco Polo
- — China's current border
- Mongol Empire
- Great Wall

Foreign influence in China

During the late Qing Dynasty, China chose to be isolated, cutting itself off from the rest of the world. But in the early 1800s, the British came to China, demanding to trade in goods such as tea, spices, silk, and porcelain. In return, the British brought a drug called **opium**. Many Chinese people became addicted to opium. When China tried to ban the drug, the British fought and won wars to continue their trade. With each defeat, China gave up further rights and territory. In 1842 the Chinese gave Britain the island of Hong Kong.

MAO ZEDONG
(1893–1976)

Mao Zedong was an important Communist Party leader during the 1930s and 1940s. When surrounded by Nationalists in 1934, Mao famously led tens of thousands of followers thousands of miles to safety. This became known as the Long March.

The Nationalists and Communists

In 1911 groups opposed to Qing leadership rose up in rebellion. Emperor Puyi was forced to give up his position as ruler in 1912. Sun Yat-sen, leader of the victorious Nationalist Party, declared China a **republic** and became its president. At the same time, a new **Communist** Party grew in opposition to the Nationalists. Communists believe the state, rather than individuals, should own and control property and resources.

Japanese invasion

In the 1930s Japanese troops invaded China, taking over Beijing in 1937. The Chinese Communists and Nationalists, led by Chiang Kai-shek, decided to work together to force out the Japanese. However, **civil war** began again in 1945 between the Nationalists and Communists.

Communist victory and the Cultural Revolution

The Communists defeated the Nationalists in 1949. Mao Zedong proclaimed the People's Republic of China and became its leader. In defeat, more than two million Nationalists followed Chiang Kai-shek to the island of Taiwan. They continued the government of the Republic of China there. Meanwhile, in 1950 Mao and the People's Republic of China invaded neighboring Tibet and took control there.

Deng Xiaoping, pictured here on a billboard, began China's "Open Door Policy," which has brought the country great wealth and increasing international power.

坚持党的基本路线一百年不动摇

In 1966 Mao began the Cultural Revolution. This was an effort to get rid of foreign influence and ancient Chinese ideas, while also strengthening Communist Party ideals. Students and young people became Red Guards, enforcing these goals. Millions of people were sentenced to forced labor, and many were tortured or killed. The Cultural Revolution ended with Mao's death in 1976.

Economic powerhouse

Deng Xiaoping became the new leader in 1978. He wanted to create a more modern China, and he encouraged private business ownership and international trade. This began China's "Open Door Policy" to the world. Over time, Deng's policies helped China's **economy** to greatly expand. In 2008 China proudly demonstrated its unity and strength by hosting the Olympic Games.

Today, China faces the challenge of a recent worldwide financial crisis. Other countries also continue to criticize China for violating human rights. Human rights are basic rights that most societies think every person should have. The Chinese government, for instance, does not protect free speech or allow free elections. Despite these ongoing challenges, China continues on its path as a world superpower.

YOUNG PEOPLE

In 1989 students gathered in Tiananmen Square in Beijing to protest government **corruption** and to call for **democracy**. After weeks of demonstrations, Chinese soldiers opened fire, killing hundreds or even thousands in the Tiananmen Square Massacre.

Regions and Resources: Great Size and Variety

China is the fourth-largest country in the world, and it has the largest population in the world. It has a long border. The East China Sea, Korea Bay, Yellow Sea, and South China Sea all border China. The countries of Afghanistan, Bhutan, Burma, India, Kazakhstan, North Korea, Kyrgyzstan, Laos, Mongolia, Nepal, Pakistan, Russia, Tajikistan, and Vietnam also border China.

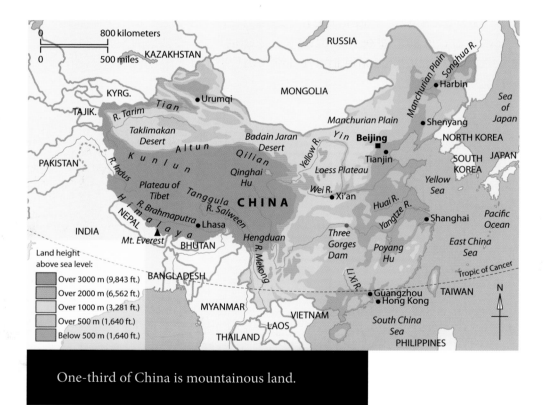

One-third of China is mountainous land.

How to say...

The name of the Yangtze River in the main language of China, Mandarin, is Changjiang. It means "long" (*chang*) "river" (*jiang*).

Chinese landscapes

China has nearly 3.7 million square miles (9.6 million square kilometers) of land. Its variety of land includes tall mountains, high **plateaus**, sandy deserts, plains, and remote forests. China's great rivers, such as the Yangtze and Yellow, have helped shape Chinese **culture**. The Yangtze is the world's third-longest river. It forms a dividing line between northern and southern China.

The tallest mountain in the world, Mount Everest, is in the Himalayan mountain range on China's border with Nepal. It reaches 29,028 feet (8,848 meters) high. At that height, the mountains are always covered with ice and snow, and thin air makes it difficult to breathe. The plateau of Tibet lies north of the Himalayas. It is sometimes called the "roof of the world."

China is a large country with a variety of beautiful natural landscapes. These bamboo rafts are floating on the Yulong River in southern China.

Climate

China has a variety of climates. Temperatures generally decrease from south to north. January is usually the coldest month, and July is the hottest. In the summer, **monsoon** winds bring rain to the south and east. China experiences frequent **typhoons** along its southern and eastern coasts. It also suffers from occasional floods, **tsunamis**, and earthquakes.

Daily Life

Fishermen on the Li River in Guilin do things the same way they have done them for hundreds of years. They guide small **bamboo** rafts using long bamboo poles. The fishermen use trained diving birds, called cormorants, to catch fish for them. The birds are treated as members of the family.

Rice paddy fields are too muddy for heavy machinery. Farmers do most of the work by hand.

China's Three Gorges Dam creates as much electricity as 15 coal-burning power plants.

Resources

China's largest lowlands are in the east around the plains and **deltas** of its major rivers. Streams and canals provide water to thousands of **paddy fields of rice**. The Chinese eat more rice than anything else, and nearly half of the population works in farming. Chinese farmers grow three rice crops a year. China is also the world's leading producer of cotton.

China's rivers provide energy in the form of **hydroelectric power**. China's Three Gorges Dam, on the Yangtze River, is the largest dam in the world. China's other natural resources include iron ore, coal, and oil. Due to its large population, the country has a huge workforce.

Industry

China has the second-largest **economy** in the world, after the United States. China makes many products, including appliances and most of the world's toys. China also produces silk, porcelain, and **lacquer**, as it has for centuries. China's economic development has been more rapid on the coasts than in the middle part of the country. About 60 percent of China's **manufacturing** comes from its east coast, with 10 percent coming from Shanghai.

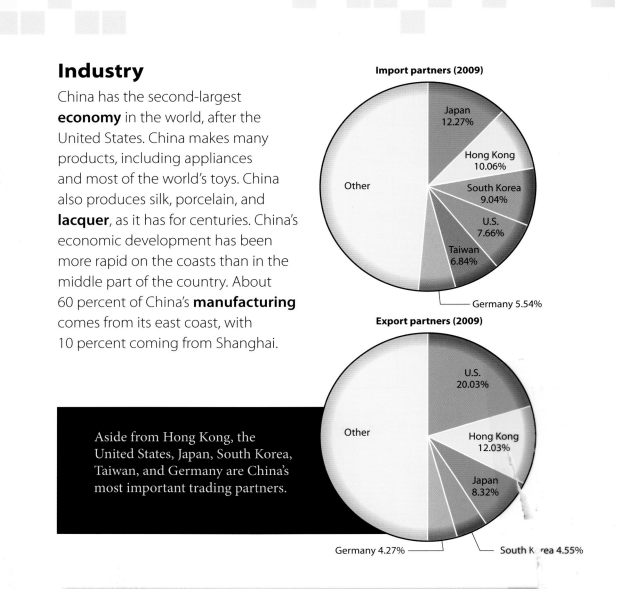

Import partners (2009)

- Japan 12.27%
- Hong Kong 10.06%
- South Korea 9.04%
- U.S. 7.66%
- Taiwan 6.84%
- Germany 5.54%
- Other

Export partners (2009)

- U.S. 20.03%
- Hong Kong 12.03%
- Japan 8.32%
- South Korea 4.55%
- Germany 4.27%
- Other

Aside from Hong Kong, the United States, Japan, South Korea, Taiwan, and Germany are China's most important trading partners.

Daily Life

Conditions and quality of life have improved for Chinese workers over the last decades. However, in 2010 China suffered **inflation**, which is a continuing increase in the price of goods. The government began to control the prices of food and energy at the end of 2010 in order to prevent protests by workers.

The Green Long March is a youth movement in China that takes action to protect the **environment**. Since 2007, youth volunteers in the Green Long March have brought attention to environmental issues. They have worked to improve water quality and to promote farming practices and energy sources that do not harm the environment.

Environmental issues

China has quickly made its economy and **industries** modern. But this has come at a price. China suffers from air and water **pollution**, **acid rain**, loss of forests, and loss of soil. China's pollution is partly due to the use of coal for most of its power. Since 2005 China has made efforts to develop "clean" energy sources, such as hydroelectric, wind, and solar power. China is also developing more **nuclear energy**.

Most of China's **exports** are manufactured goods. This woman is at work in an electronics factory.

Wildlife: Pandas, Bamboo, and More

China's **habitats** include deserts, mountains, grasslands, pine forests, and **rain forests**. China is home to thousands of **species** of plants and animals.

Some animals found in China, such as the snow leopard and giant panda, are extremely rare. Experts believe there are only about 2,000 snow leopards left in China, and there are only about 1,600 giant pandas. Most of these animals are now protected and live in **reserves** set up by the government. The giant panda has become a symbol of China. The country works with zoos around the world to breed pandas and to make sure the animal will exist in the future.

Giant pandas sometimes eat **bamboo** for 16 hours a day to get the nutrition they need.

Animals

Other creatures unique to China are the golden-haired monkey, South China tiger, and Yangtze (or Chinese) river dolphin. All of these species are also **endangered**, or at risk. The Yangtze river dolphin may now even have died out. Other at-risk animals found in China include the Yangtze alligator, wild yak, Manchurian (Siberian) tiger, brown-eared pheasant, and Asian elephant.

Animal habitats

In Tibet, snow leopards live in the remote, frozen, rugged mountains. Yaks also live on the snowy **plateau** there. Gazelles make their homes in the grasslands between Tibet and Mongolia. Goat-like animals called *takin* graze in the slopes of the Himalayas. The golden-haired monkey ranges from the high mountain forests of Sichuan **Province** to the Tibetan border.

Giant pandas live in the forested mountains of southwest China. The Chinese alligator lives in the eastern marshlands of China. The pine forests of northeast China are home to bears, caribou, elk, deer, and Siberian tigers.

The Chinese white dolphin can be seen on the southeast coast of China. It is a rare dolphin that is sometimes pink in color.

Environmental conservation

China now has more than 1,200 reserves to protect its wild creatures and habitats. Reserves currently protect more than 15 percent of China's land, and there are plans for more reserves in the future.

The leaves on a gingko tree turn a golden yellow before falling off in the chill of autumn.

Plants

China has around 30,000 plant species. Some of China's most important plants and trees are bamboo, tea, gingko, the dawn redwood, and orchids. Also important are the numerous plants used for medicine.

Bamboo is light, strong, and flexible, and it can be used to build many things. The gingko is considered a living fossil because it is the last of a type of plant that lived 300 million years ago. Gingko trees are now planted around the world because they can survive in cold conditions and in cities. The dawn redwood tree is also considered a living fossil, and it is unique to China.

Cactus plants survive in the harsh Taklimakan Desert. The far south of China has rain forests with thousands of varieties of plants. Hundreds of wildflowers can be seen in bloom in Yunnan Province.

These are lotus flowers in bloom in China's spring months.

Infrastructure:
A Communist State

China is a **communist** state. Communist states own the country's property and businesses and set prices and salaries. In China, however, the government allows some private ownership of businesses, and it encourages profit and the increase of individual wealth. At the same time, the Chinese government maintains overall control of the **economy**.

Regions

China is divided into 22 **provinces**. It claims Taiwan as a 23rd province. Hong Kong and Macau are considered "special administrative regions." They have local assemblies and more self-government. The British returned Hong Kong to China in 1997. The Portuguese returned Macau to China in 1999.

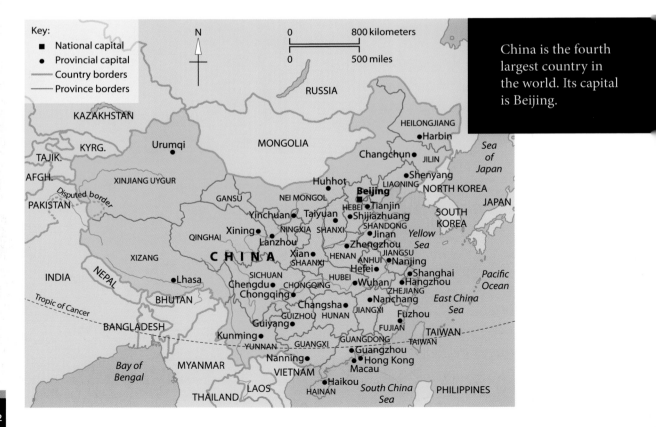

Key:
- ■ National capital
- ● Provincial capital
- — Country borders
- — Province borders

N

0   800 kilometers
0   500 miles

China is the fourth largest country in the world. Its capital is Beijing.

KAZAKHSTAN

RUSSIA

HEILONGJIANG
●Harbin

KYRG.   Urumqi   MONGOLIA   Sea
TAJIK.   ●   Changchun● JILIN   of
AFGH.   ●Shenyang   Japan
              XINJIANG UYGUR   Huhhot● LIAONING NORTH KOREA
PAKISTAN   GANSU   NEI MONGOL   Beijing■   JAPAN
                      Yinchuan● Taiyuan HEBEI●Tianjin
                              ●   ●Shijiazhuang SOUTH
                  Xining● NINGXIA SHANXI SHANDONG KOREA
         QINGHAI   ●Lanzhou   ●Jinan Yellow
                                    ●Zhengzhou Sea
    XIZANG   C H I N A Xian● HENAN JIANGSU
                         SHAANXI ANHUI ●Nanjing
INDIA   NEPAL   Hefei●   ●Shanghai   Pacific
                  SICHUAN   HUBEI   ●Hangzhou   Ocean
         ●Lhasa Chengdu● CHONGQING ●Wuhan ZHEJIANG
              BHUTAN Chongqing●   ●Nanchang East China
Tropic of Cancer   Changsha● JIANGXI   Fuzhou   Sea
                      GUIZHOU HUNAN   FUJIAN
BANGLADESH   Guiyang●   TAIWAN
              Kunming●   GUANGXI GUANGDONG TAIWAN
         YUNNAN   Nanning● ●Guangzhou
    Bay of   MYANMAR   ●●Hong Kong
    Bengal   VIETNAM   Macau
              LAOS   ●Haikou South China PHILIPPINES
         THAILAND HAINAN   Sea

These two Uyghur girls are reading together. The Uyghur are one of the major ethnic groups in China.

People and language

Over 90 percent of Chinese people are from the Han ethnic group. Other major ethnic groups include Tibetans, Dai, and Uyghurs. Aside from the Han, the People's **Republic** of China recognizes 55 other ethnic groups, which together number over 100 million people.

There are different languages in China, as well as different dialects (slightly different versions of a language). Mandarin is the official language and the most widely spoken. Cantonese is spoken only in the south.

Government

The Chinese Communist Party dominates China's government. Most officials are appointed rather than elected, or chosen by the people. The general secretary of the Chinese Communist Party runs the government as its president. Hu Jintao has been president since March 2003.

The National People's Congress makes up the legislative (law-making) branch. Regional people's congresses and the People's Liberation Army (PLA) elect the members. The Supreme People's Court tops China's judicial branch, with judges appointed by the National People's Congress.

Chinese students do group exercises every morning.

One-child policy

With a large population and limited resources, China has struggled to manage its food supply and quality of life for its people. Beginning in 1978, the Chinese government promoted a policy of a one-child family among the Han (the majority ethnic group). This has begun to reduce the rate at which China's population grew. China has relaxed this policy in recent years, however.

Education

Most Chinese children begin attending school at around age six. China's education system includes six years of grade school (primary school), six years of secondary school (like middle school and high school), and four years of university education. The government pays for basic education for everyone, but not higher education.

Children in the cities tend to get a better education than children outside the cities. However, recent efforts are changing that. Almost all children in China now attend grade school. School is usually held six days a week. Chinese children often feel a great deal of pressure to succeed in school if they are the only child in the family.

The drawing of Chinese characters is an ancient art form in China.

YOUNG PEOPLE

At school, children learn to spell out Chinese words phonetically (as they sound) using a system called Pinyin. They also learn Chinese script, which is made up of a set of over 40,000 unique characters. Yet, most university-educated Chinese people know only between 3,000 and 4,000 characters.

Chinese children learn the Chinese and English languages in school. They also learn math, science, history, geography, music, and art, and they do physical education. School lasts from before 8 a.m. to 4 p.m. Many students then go to an after-school program until their parents finish the workday.

Moving people

China's population continues to increase. The trend in recent years in China has been for younger people to move east to cities on the coast. These young people are looking for jobs and opportunities.

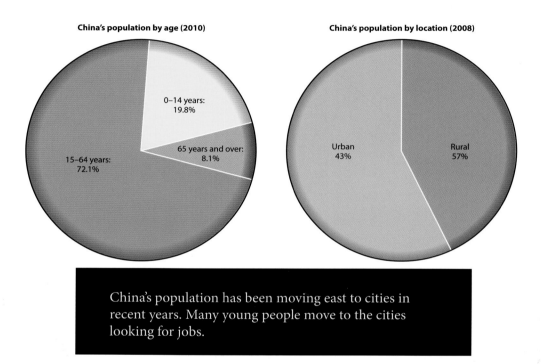

China's population by age (2010)

0–14 years:
19.8%

15–64 years:
72.1%

65 years and over:
8.1%

China's population by location (2008)

Urban
43%

Rural
57%

China's population has been moving east to cities in recent years. Many young people move to the cities looking for jobs.

The easiest way to travel around China is by train. Poor roads in some areas can make it difficult to travel by car. Within China's cities, most people get around by bicycle or on foot. However, an increasing number of people in China are buying cars and flying, as the government invests in new roads and airports.

Health care

China is one of the most rapidly aging countries in the world, and this will certainly put a strain on its healthcare system. Many people in China still practice traditional Chinese medicine, which seeks a balance of **yin and yang** in the body. Combinations of herbs brewed into soup or tea are given to cure various illnesses and restore balance.

Recent developments

In 2009 the worldwide financial crisis reduced the demand for Chinese **exports** after many years of growth. The government is now trying to make China less dependent on exports. Overall, China continues to have an increasing international influence.

YOUNG PEOPLE

The Young Pioneers are similar to the Boy Scouts or Girl Scouts. Children in the Young Pioneers wear a red neckerchief, which is a piece of cloth tied around the neck like a scarf. Young Pioneers are supposed to represent the Communist Party traits of bravery, initiative (taking it upon yourself to do something), and self-sacrifice.

Young Chinese boys and girls sometimes join the Young Pioneers as an activity.

Culture: Ancient and Rich

China has one of the oldest **cultures** in the world, with history and traditions dating back thousands of years. China's variety of festivals, arts, philosophies, and other traditions were abandoned in the 1960s and 1970s during the Cultural Revolution. Today, however, the Chinese are again proud to celebrate their rich traditions and share them with the world.

Holidays and festivals

Chinese New Year, also called Spring Festival, is a national holiday. During the dragon dance, people in long, colorful dragon costumes move rhythmically through crowded streets. Fireworks, which are a Chinese invention, pop as the new **lunar** year begins.

China has several other national holidays (see page 38). Popular traditional holidays include the Lantern Festival, during which people display colorful lanterns at night.

Chinese celebrate their new year with parades.

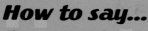

Traditional Chinese opera costumes are works of art in themselves.

Music

Modern Chinese composers combine traditional Chinese instruments with modern sounds. Even though Mandarin is the official language of China, Chinese pop music is dominated by "Cantopop," in which singers use the Cantonese language. Singers Aaron Kwok, Andy Lau, Jacky Cheung, and Leon Lai are called the "Four Kings of Cantopop."

China's long musical tradition includes Chinese opera, which is a form of theater. It is still performed today and is one of China's most popular forms of entertainment. The art dates back to the 700s. Performers wear colorful, very detailed costumes and makeup.

Art and calligraphy

Nature, rather than people, is usually the focus of Chinese painting. The balance of **yin and yang** is always a consideration in Chinese art, as it is in many parts of Chinese life. Many traditional Chinese paintings also include writing, or inscriptions, of Chinese characters. Chinese **calligraphy** is an important art, requiring great skill with a brush. China has a rich tradition of writing, including poems dating back thousands of years.

Philosophy and religion

China has no official religion, but **Buddhism** is popular among the Chinese. Buddhism originally came from India around 2,000 years ago. The philosophies (systems of ideas and thoughts) called Taoism (or Daoism) and Confucianism started in China.

Taoism rejects aggression, material goods, and social status and seeks a balanced, peaceful existence. Confucianism refers to the thinking and teachings of the ancient philosopher Confucius. He encouraged a respect of elders and the idea that one's actions always affect others.

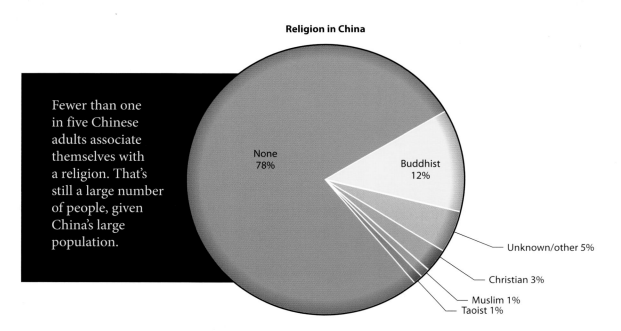

Religion in China

None 78%

Buddhist 12%

Unknown/other 5%

Christian 3%

Muslim 1%

Taoist 1%

Fewer than one in five Chinese adults associate themselves with a religion. That's still a large number of people, given China's large population.

People practice kung fu and Tai Chi in parks around China.

Sports

Soccer and ping-pong, or table tennis, are the most popular sports in China. Chinese players usually dominate table tennis at the Olympic Games and international competitions. China usually does very well in the Olympics in general, winning many medals. Other popular sports include badminton, acrobatics, and gymnastics.

Martial arts

Gongfu, or kung fu, is one of the most famous Chinese inventions and sports. It is based on animal movements and is meant to improve a person's body and mind, in addition to offering physical protection and warrior skills. Tai Chi is another Chinese martial art and exercise that has become popular all over the world.

Movies and television

Some recent movies from China have become famous worldwide, including *Crouching Tiger, Hidden Dragon* and *Hero*. In general, Chinese movies are limited by government **censorship**. However, there is also a well-known Hong Kong film **industry**, producing actors such as Jet Li and Jackie Chan.

China Central Television, or CCTV, is the major television broadcaster in China, with around 20 channels. Chinese soap operas are popular. CCTV reports directly to the **Communist** Party, which determines its programming and uses it for **propaganda**. The government must approve foreign-made programs before they are broadcast.

China has a long tradition of kite-flying.

Fun and games

Kites, tops, and yo-yos all came from China. Kite-flying is popular, and some Chinese kites are works of art. Stamp collecting is another common Chinese hobby.

Food

The Chinese use chopsticks and spoons to eat their meals, but they do not use knives at the table. Chinese cooking uses many spices and ingredients, such as ginger, garlic, chili peppers, cinnamon, pepper, sesame oil, mushrooms, soy sauce, and vinegar. Tea is very popular in China.

Moon cakes

Chinese moon cakes are eaten on Chinese New Year, which is based on the lunar (moon) calendar. They are a dessert-like treat that look like the moon. Sometimes moon cakes are fancy, with impressions of Chinese characters (letters) on them. When making this treat, make sure an adult helps you to use the oven.

Ingredients

¼ cup sugar
2 egg yolks
½ cup salted butter
1 cup all-purpose flour

1 cup red bean paste, or your favorite fruit jam

What to do

1. Preheat the oven to 375°F (190°C).

2. Combine the sugar, one egg yolk, and butter. Stir.

3. Mix in the flour to make the dough.

4. Form the dough into a large ball and wrap it in plastic wrap.

5. Refrigerate the dough for 30 minutes.

6. Unwrap the chilled dough and form small balls by rolling it between the palms of your hands.

7. Make an indentation in the center of each moon cake and fill it with about ½ teaspoon of bean paste or jam.

8. Beat the remaining egg yolk and brush it onto each moon cake.

9. Place the moon cakes on a cookie sheet and bake for about 20 minutes, or until the outside edges are slightly brown.

China Today

The streets of China's cities are much like those of any other modern city around the world. People chat busily on cell phones while looking in store windows. Others drive by in new cars, while a skyscraper construction project continues nearby. At the same time, a small group of people may be practicing Tai Chi in a city park. Businesspeople might be having a snack of traditional Chinese steamed dumplings. The mix of ancient and modern is part of what makes China special.

China's **economy** has seen tremendous growth over the past decades, as it has embraced private business ownership and wealth. Economic success has given China a greater role in international affairs. It has also led to a higher standard of living for most Chinese people.

China's challenges

The challenges facing China today are many. A downturn in **exports** affected China's economy in 2010. China continues to face the challenge of feeding its population of over one billion people. **Pollution** continues to be a problem, as China works to move toward cleaner energy, with projects such as the Three Gorges Dam.

As its power has grown, so has international pressure for China to improve its human rights record (see page 11). The **communist** government remains firmly in control. Chinese people who speak out loudly in disagreement with government policies are often jailed.

As Chinese citizens continue to become more familiar with foreign goods and ideas, it will be interesting to see how things develop. The Chinese government will need to seek a balance to keep its tight controls, satisfy its people, and take a greater role in maintaining international peace and stability.

Some Chinese cities, such as Suzhou, are as fast-paced and modern as New York City or London.

Fact File

Official name: People's **Republic** of China

Official language: Mandarin Chinese

Capital city: Beijing

Bordering countries: Afghanistan, Bhutan, Burma, India, Kazakhstan, North Korea, Kyrgyzstan, Laos, Mongolia, Nepal, Pakistan, Russia, Tajikistan, Vietnam

Population: 1,330,141,295* (July 2010 est.) (*greatest in the world)

Largest cities (populations): Shanghai (15,789,000)
Beijing (11,741,000)
Guangzhou (9,447,000)

System of government: **Communist** state

Date of independence: October 1, 1949 (People's Republic of China established)

These Buddhist monks are gathered for prayer at Jade Buddha Temple in Shanghai.

Religions: China is officially atheist, a belief that God does not exist.

Life expectancy: 74.51 years

Literacy rate: 91.6 percent

Area (total): 3,694,959 square miles (9,569,901 square kilometers)

Average temperature: 53°F (11.8°C)

Highest elevation: Mount Everest, 29,035 feet (8,850 meters)

Lowest elevation: Turpan Pendi Depression, Xinjiang, 505 feet (154 meters) below sea level

Longest river: Yangtze, 3,915 miles (6,300 kilometers)

Largest lakes: Poyang (freshwater), Qinghai (saltwater)

Local currency: Renminbi (also called yuan)

Resources: Coal, iron ore, petroleum (oil), natural gas, mercury, tin, aluminum, lead, zinc, rare earth elements, uranium, other minerals and metals, **hydroelectric power**

Exports: Electrical and other machinery (including data processing equipment), apparel, textiles, iron and steel, optical and medical equipment

Imports: Electrical and other machinery, oil and mineral fuels, optical and medical equipment, metal ores, plastics, organic chemicals

Trading partners: United States, Hong Kong, Japan, South Korea, Germany, Taiwan

National animal:	Giant panda
National symbol:	Chinese dragon
National fruit:	Kiwifruit
Famous Chinese people:	Confucius (551–479 BCE), philosopher
	Deng Xiaoping (1904–1997), Communist leader
	Gong Li (born 1965), actress
	Jackie Chan (1954), martial arts film star
	Lang Lang (born 1982), musician
	Li Na (born 1982), tennis player
	Mao Zedong (1893–1976), Communist Party leader
	Qin Shi Huangdi (259–210 BCE), first **emperor** of China
	Tan Dun (born 1957), composer/conductor
	Zhang Yimou (born 1950), filmmaker

National holidays:	January 1	New Year's Day
		Chinese New Year (takes place in January or February, depending on the **lunar** calendar)
	March 8	International Women's Day
	May 1	International Labor Day
	May 4	Youth Day
	June 1	Children's Day
	July 1	Communist Party Birthday
	August 1	Army Day
	October 1	National Day (Anniversary of the founding of the People's Republic of China)

National anthem
"Yiyonggjun Jinxingqu"
("The March of the Volunteers")

Arise, ye who refuse to be slaves!
With our flesh and blood, let us build our new Great Wall!
The Chinese nation faces its greatest danger.
From each one the urgent call for action comes forth.
Arise! Arise! Arise!
Millions with but one heart,
Braving the enemy's fire.
March on!
Braving the enemy's fire.
March on! March on! March on!

Fishermen on the Li River guide small rafts using **bamboo** poles. They use diving birds, called cormorants, to catch fish for them.

Timeline

BCE means Before the Common Era. When this appears after a date, it refers to the number of years before the Christian religion began. BCE dates are always counted backward.

CE means Common Era. When this appears after a date, it refers to the time after the Christian religion began.

BCE

c. 5000–3000	The Yangshao **culture** enjoys success in northern China.
1700s	The Shang **Dynasty** develops.
1046–256	The Zhou Dynasty rules China.
551–479	The Chinese philosopher Confucius is alive.
221	China is united under the Qin Dynasty. Construction begins on the Great Wall.
150	**Buddhism** is introduced to China from India.

CE

618–907	The Tang Dynasty rules, and the arts flourish.
1209	Genghis Khan unites the **Mongols** and invades northern China.
1279	Mongol leader Kublai Khan establishes the Yuan Dynasty.
1368	The Ming Dynasty is established after the Ming overthrow the Mongols.
1417	Construction of the Forbidden City (in today's Beijing) begins.
1839	The First **Opium** War begins after the Chinese government attempts to stop the British opium trade.
1842	The Treaty of Nanjing gives Hong Kong to Great Britain.

1900	The Boxer Rebellion takes place, when Westerners and Christians in China are attacked and killed.
1911	Chinese revolutionaries overthrow the Qing Dynasty.
1912	Sun Yat-sen becomes president of the Chinese **Republic**.
1921	The Chinese **Communist** Party is founded.
1931	Japan invades Manchuria, and fighting breaks out between China and Japan.
1945–1949	Chinese Nationalists and Communists fight in a **civil war**.
1949	Communist leader Mao Zedong forms the People's Republic of China. Chiang Kai-shek's Nationalists retreat to Taiwan and set up the Republic of China.
1966	The Cultural Revolution begins.
1976	Mao Zedong dies.
1978	Deng Xiaoping wins control of the government and begins reforms that open up China to the rest of the world.
1979	China enacts the "One-Child Family Campaign" to help limit population growth.
1989	The Chinese army opens fire on protesters of government corruption in Beijing's Tiananmen Square, killing many.
1997	Great Britain returns control of Hong Kong to China.
1999	Portugal returns control of Macau to China.
2003	The Three Gorges Dam begins to generate electricity.
2008	An earthquake, killing thousands, hits the Sichuan **Province**. Beijing hosts the Olympic Games.
2009	China relaxes its strictly enforced one-child policy, and officials in Shanghai urge parents to have a second child to help counter the effects of China's aging population.

Glossary

acid rain rain that contains harmful acid caused by chemicals in the air

bamboo light, strong, and flexible plant used to build many things

Buddhism religion originated in India by Buddha (Siddhartha Gautama)

calligraphy beautiful penmanship, especially highly decorative handwriting

censorship practice of examining books, films, television, and so on, in order to remove anything considered harmful or dangerous

civil war war between groups within the same country

communist person or country that practices a social system in which all people share work and property; also used to describe the Communist Party in China

corruption dishonest or illegal behavior or misuse of power

culture practices, beliefs, and traditions of a society

currency bills and coins accepted in return for goods and services

delta coastal area of low land where a river spreads out and meets the sea

democracy system in which every citizen of a country can vote to elect government officials

dynasty series of rulers from the same family or group

economy having to do with the money, industries, and jobs in a country

emperor person who rules over an empire, which is a group of countries

endangered something in danger of being destroyed

environment natural world, including plants and animals

export to ship goods to other countries for sale or exchange

habitat environment where a plant or animal is found

hydroelectric power energy generated using the power of moving water

industry having to do with large-scale production and business

inflation continuing or rapid increase in prices of goods

lacquer liquid painted onto wood to form a hard, polished surface

lunar relating to the moon

manufacturing business of making goods in factories

Mongol member of a group of skilled horsemen and warriors from the grasslands north of China

monsoon season of heavy rain

nuclear energy energy produced when the nucleus of an atom is split

opium powerful, addictive drug made from poppy seeds

paddy field land that is flooded so rice can be grown there

plateau large, flat area of highland

pollution addition of harmful gases or chemicals to the environment, for example, to the air or water

propaganda information, ideas, or rumors spread widely to help or harm a person, group, movement, institution, nation, and so on

province specific region within a country

rain forest tropical forest with dense growth and high annual rainfall

republic independent country with a head of government who is not a king or queen

reserve area set aside to protect wildlife

species particular type of animal or plant

subarctic related to an area near the Arctic region, immediately south of the Arctic Circle

subtropical related to an area near a tropical region, characterized by warm, humid weather

tsunami very large wave, usually caused by an underwater earthquake, that can cause tremendous damage when it reaches land

typhoon powerful storm that forms over tropical waters in parts of the Pacific Ocean; in other regions, it is called a hurricane or tropical cyclone

yin and yang two forces that the ancient Chinese believed influence everything in the universe; yin is dark and represents the female, and yang is light and represents the male

Find Out More

Books

Block, Marta Segal, and Charlotte Guillain. *China Focus* (series). Chicago: Heinemann Library, 2008.

Conyers, Karen Elizabeth. *Teens in China (Global Connections)*. Minneapolis: Compass Point, 2008.

Green, Jen. *China (Countries of the World)*. Washington, D.C.: National Geographic, 2009.

Kalman, Bobbie. *China: The Land (Lands, Peoples, and Cultures)*. New York: Crabtree, 2008.

McCulloch, Julie. *China (A World of Recipes)*. Chicago: Heinemann Library, 2009.

Riehecky, Janet. *China (Country Explorers)*. Minneapolis: Lerner, 2008.

Sebag-Montefiore, Poppy. *China (Eyewitness)*. New York: DK Children, 2007.

Websites

https://www.cia.gov/library/publications/the-world-factbook/index. html

The World Factbook provides information on the history, people, government, geography, and more of China and over 250 other nations.

www.who.int/countries/chn/en/

The website of the World Health Organization (WHO) provides health information concerning China.

http://portal.unesco.org/ci/en/ev.php-URL_ID=1338&URL_DO=DO_ TOPIC&URL_SECTION=201.html

You can learn about China's involvement with the United Nations Educational, Scientific, and Cultural Organization (UNESCO).

http://unstats.un.org/unsd/default.htm

This United Nations site offers links to a range of statistics on China and other countries.

Places to visit

If you are lucky enough to visit China, here are some places you could visit:

The Forbidden City, Beijing
The Forbidden City is the best-preserved collection of imperial architecture in China.

Museum of Terracotta Warriors and Horses, near Xi'an
Emperor Qin Shi Huangdi ordered the creation of the terracotta army, which was buried for over 2,000 years before being discovered by a farmer in 1974.

The Great Wall
The Great Wall winds across China for over 4,000 miles (6,700 kilometers).

Yangtze River and Three Gorges Dam
A tour boat can be taken down the Yangtze River to see the Three Gorges Dam, which is the world's largest dam and the world's largest hydroelectric power plant.

Jiuzhaigou, Sichuan Province
Jiuzhaigou Valley is a nature reserve famous for its lakes and waterfalls.

Potala Palace, Lhasa, Tibetan Autonomous Region
The Potala Palace is now a museum, but it is traditionally the seat of the Dalai Lama, who is the spiritual leader of Tibetan Buddhists.

Wolong Nature Reserve, outside Chengdu
The Wolong Nature Preserve is the largest giant panda reserve in China.

Hong Kong
Hong Kong is a good place to see the cutting edge of Chinese and Asian society. The Kowloon side promenade allows a view of some of the great modern architecture of China.

Topic Tools

You can use these topic tools for your school projects. Trace the flag and map on to a sheet of paper, using the thick black outlines to guide you, then color in your pictures. Make sure you use the right colors for the flag!

In the flag of the People's Republic of China, the color red represents revolution. The small stars symbolize the traditional social classes of the Chinese people. The small stars also represent the people of China, who are united around the large star, which represents the Communist Party of China.

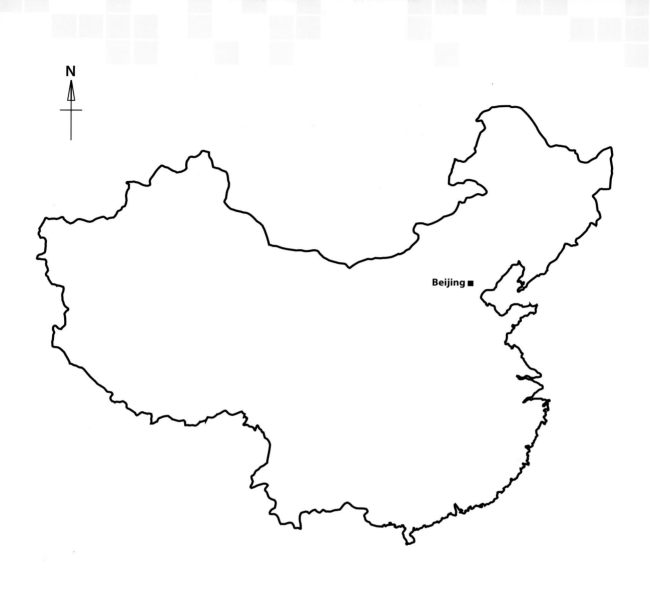

Beijing ■

Index

Titles in the series